SONGS FOR THE LONG NIGHT.

SONGS FOR THE LONG NIGHT.
BY KORBIN JONES

A Rebel Satori Imprint

New Orleans

Published in the United States of America by
REBEL SATORI PRESS
www.rebelsatoripress.com

Copyright © 2019 by Korbin Jones. All rights reserved. Except for brief passages quoted in newspaper, magazine, radio, television, or online reviews, no part of this book may be reproduced in any form or any means, electronic or mechanical, including photocopying, recording, or information or retrieval system, without the permission in writing from the publisher. Please do not participate in or encourage piracy of copyrighted materials in violation of the author's rights. Purchase only authorized editions.

Cover Art: Emily Bunch

TABLE OF CONTENTS

prelude.	1
hymn for brown-eyed boys.	2
carpenters.	3
the flowers pay witness to us.	4
and the wind whispered them away.	5
we inherited their mistakes.	7
inconsistencies: number five.	9
holy friday morning bathed in light.	10
departure.	11
men to my father.	12
transfiguration.	16
inconsistencies: number four.	17
bereavement: part one.	18
against the moonlight.	19
man, exposed.	20
gospel according to saint sebastian.	22
bereavement: part two.	24
inconsistencies: number one.	25
the water between us.	26
rehearsed visitation.	27
better is relative.	28
freshening.	29
bereavement: part three.	30
the complete history of us.	31
interlude.	32
inconsistencies: number three.	33
meaning revelation or unveiling.	36
vivisection.	37
entry for trauma relived.	38
seeds & skin.	40
inconsistencies: number two.	41

i'll name her something soft.	43
lockjaw.	44
tea leaf apostle.	47
growth rate.	49
pink.	50
milk settles on the tongue.	52
gifting my father a second birth.	54
fallen.	56
apostasy: instructions for getting over me.	58
liminal spaces.	61
inconsistencies: number six.	63
prayer for saint kathie.	67
séance.	68
light in the stairwell.	70
postlude.	72
notes	75
acknowledgements	77
gratitudes	78

PRELUDE.

i've fastened you to the countless ways
i procrastinate.

but i've planned this all out, sipping coke
on the southern bank

as you make my legs into spires
for the coming church on this river.

you say the sun serves up
my eyes well, and i laugh,

the carbonation dancing in the glasses
held close to our mouths—

mine: soft. yours: bearded.
the workers will come in the morning,

their hardhats the color of sunlit waters,
our bodies still busied with the canon.

HYMN FOR BROWN-EYED BOYS.

on the day of our awakening,
god put melanin in the eyes
of men, deep and dark like
my love for them—
then took it away,
called these blue eyes better,
said absence is beautiful,
then gave us cataracts.
same song, second verse,
a gospel according to
willow-bodied white boys.
but i've come to know
your eyes by moonlight—
staring at them and not
the ceiling, how they break
and bid my heart come tighter.
these baby blues got nothing on
you, got nothing on the color
my ancestors saw for
generations above them,
backs laid flat against the earth,
making love and constellations
out of night, making gold
out of eyes that would lead us
to pluck out our own.

CARPENTERS.

see the bearded man wrapped halfway 'round the lamp post
in the park, burning bright like dragon's breath.
see his artist fingers and imagine the way he paints
between my teeth—nail under incisor, eyes toward heaven.
our bodies carving the bed like wood, our sweat as varnish,
blinds open and on display without knowing.
sheets white and damp like canvas before the first stroke.
knuckles pressed white against the lamp post—a spotlight
for this exhibition of sex and breathing and we,
this walking spectacle, are erotic as dragonflies clutched in flight.

THE FLOWERS PAY WITNESS TO US.

tonight: our bodies forgive
the wilting flowers on the nightstand,
forget the heated argument, and now—
as your body moves on mine
like hungry vines on tooth-cut ruins—
i see an honesty in your eyes,
as if you've been staring
into the mouth of unprecedence
and found it worthy of a risk,
of a kiss, of a first time for everything
in a stranger's bed.
the rose you gave me is pressed
inside an encyclopedia of fairytales,
somewhere near the end between
several sheets of cheap paper towels
to absorb the pink moisture,
to keep the letters from running.
it will be dried soon, the book
warped from its presence.

AND THE WIND WHISPERED THEM AWAY.

i'm bowed behind you, a crescent-shaped man
against which you lie, as you tell your mother
that her unconditional love seems less so and
it's the denial that hurts you most—
the required rebreaking, resetting, and recasting
of this broken bone that was ivory and smooth
'til someone saw it as a bit curved—
and thus we reached this cycle and
at what point will the bone stop mending
itself from strain, fatigue, and stress?

breaks and fractures lead to tougher tissues after healing—
so, one day that bone may become resilient to snapping
by the hands of others and then its little crooked self
won't seem to be in need of fixing anymore.

the window is open as it's summer and comforting.
a man outside is making good work of the lawn.the blades of grass have
      grown tipped and their heights
varied as they have yet to meet the blades
of a mower or weedeater but now it comes—
and now the hum of yardwork sounds like nothing more
than forced conformity because what would
the neighbors think? the drivers in their cars

as they glance over on their ways to work or home—
and what would they say?

when you finally fall asleep and the man is done outside
i can just make out the sighs of wind as they cause
the shutters to clatter softly against themselves.
when i leave there is no evidence or reconciliation.

WE INHERITED THEIR MISTAKES.

and in the slumped archways of the missions
where not my fathers, but their cousins
stripped the people bear to boiled-white bones,
his mother found me coiled around a man,
her son, and looked at me, bad as a mirror.

the river watched us from below, cradled
by the valley that had witnessed the bleaching
of unknowable masses by god held in
the mouths of men, in the mouth of his mother,
and like a sudden gust—it is my father's.

memories of that bare evening bring the river
to its knees, snaps it at the neck. the night
my father cast me out into the sleeping bodies
of pigs, drove me to the water's edge,
floating down to that land without evil.

with a rushing out and calls to god, his mother
set the table, lit the candles, called a woman
whose ear was pressed to the virgin's mouth.
she'd gone to her before, each time her son
confessed himself like an open wound.

yet in the lamplight of her bedroom she
forgets him, cleanses her memories with salt
until she sees him new, wrapped up in
the fragrant cloths she first held him in,
until she can forgive herself for listening.

INCONSISTENCIES: NUMBER FIVE.

let me kiss your every part, starting with what
your mother fashioned first of you in utero—
before the eyes you undressed me with the night
we met, before the hands you use to admire
my own mother's handiwork. before a semblance
of heart or brain drifted through her amniotic fluid,
thick and sweet with loving you before knowing you.

you, named *deuterostome*, meaning *second mouth* in greek.
meaning this parted mouth of mine was all but first,
the younger dent, so let it serve your first one well,
let it become a throne for the first born, rightful heir,
whose network of nerves are slick against my tongue,
paying homage to you and only you, my gaping maw
ushering you open, singing *hallelujah* in silence.

HOLY FRIDAY MORNING BATHED IN LIGHT.

those quiet breaths upon the pillow.
the gentle cadence of his lungs
expanding and collapsing before me.
this is seeing god, outside of
burning bushes and over-cooked toast.
this is tasting faith on his exhales—
gone too soon to commit to memory,
yet knowing that, at one point, i had tasted it,
felt it real enough to offer up a hallelujah,
and when he goes in the morning,
dressed in everything but my goodbye,
i'll lose this ability to speak in tongues
outside his arms and in the unforgiving light
because his holy spirit is a movement, not
a foundation to build my church upon.

DEPARTURE.

he's stained as a jewel is—
as a glass window in a church is.
here, in the early morning airport,
the glass is clear—why I see him
so clear. skin blanched to honey agate.
tired eyes like old peaches, wrinkled
and smaller as i continue down the line.
the immigration officer asks me
for my passport. its leather cover slips
from between my thumb and pointer,
and when he stamps it red i take it back
and look again. he's looking, too—
face half-eclipsed by his mother's shoulder
as frostbite gnaws at his nose,
his lips—wet like leaving, wet like my eyes
as the glass frosts over. i shoulder
my bags and tear myself from
the three-month-long goodbye.

MEN TO MY FATHER.

father, let me tell you about them all:

the first time was at his place.
my first everything with a man—
kiss. touch. delayed rape.

on a sunday.

his bear trap hands
on my surrendered legs.

when i stumbled home
and turned the couch
into a deathbed
you changed the channel.

the second man put aching
in my jaw. never before
had i felt like a serpent.

mouth unhinged. welcoming.
body cold from all the dark.
yet my tongue stayed still,
could not lick out a simple *no*.

bent by piety.
bent by being desired.
but now i say it all to you.

the third was prolonged,
a bender that turned me
inside out. fucked me drunk

until he saw the tears.
said they were ugly.

stepped through my open doors.
half my fault, i reasoned.

i crept out in darkness,
went to buy a test. two.
would've bought more
if i'd had the money.

negative. negative.
yet no peace came.
there were never enough.

i wrapped them up
in trash bags, prayed
you wouldn't go digging.

the fourth man you guessed at,
forbade but it was too late.

the night before:
our movements were hushed
by the burnt gunpowder
of your feet downstairs.

half past two.

when i saw him next,
it was love and spite
that laid me down
beside him, a state away,
the third weekend in a row.

the central air hummed,
cooled our skin
and covered the singing
of his body gliding
over mine, our breathing.
i hope it crossed
your mind, made you lose
a bit of sleep.

we did not stop,
did not rest.

welcomed the sun
through the shades
with our bodies—
briars in a twisted heap.

TRANSFIGURATION.

in this dream, you shine in the waters—
your scales like pennies, copper to my silver.
in this land, years ago, men mined for
metals and came up broke. there's hunger now,
starving, so we swim close together, our bodies
brushing to the point of mild agitation,
an occasional scale loosed and lost to the currents.
we survive like this for months, the river
quiet and cold, and then one day you see
the shimmer of gold high-up, above the surface.
for a moment, you leave a fin's length between us,
and the gold comes down on you like lightning.
i smell the blood first, iron sacrament, looking
just in time to see your figure hoisted by
the fisherman's spear, the quick undulation
of your body, a final goodbye as you ascend
and are eaten by air. i wake up choking on it.

INCONSISTENCIES: NUMBER FOUR.

the way a mantis shrimp
bangs its claws against the water.
makes lightning in a bubble.
stuns with just one hit.
the coral watches all in awe,
cast every shade of pink
before the bleaching.
if this were love, the beast
would be less hungry,
always fed, yet strike as often,
leave a reef of broken bodies
in the sand—fins tangled up
in seaweed, eyes like pearls,
glazed over. the echo of chewing
can be heard from deep
within the hunter's burrow—
the same sound of you breathing
beside me in the night.

BEREAVEMENT: PART ONE.

he has yet to place his heart—
the whole thing—under a microscope.
each time he tries, the eyepiece punctures
a wall, causes blood to seep and smudge the lens.
thinking he was revolutionary, he attached it
to a rocket pointed at the moon,
but his heart came loose somewhere between
and when he tried to observe it through
a telescope, all he saw was the moon
and her black hair. he spent the rest of the night
with his eye stuck to the sky, hoping for a bloody streak,
fooling himself more than once into believing
he saw it in a red star, later—mars, not folding up
until the sun stole all the night. some books
say he later threw himself into the river, drinking
it in until his chest was full again, but i think
he never did look for the heart, afraid he would see
it beating, coated in moondust, so he ate rocks
just to feel full, his lips covered in limestone,
until he himself was earth.

AGAINST THE MOONLIGHT.

i eat the rest of my birthday cake a week later in the dark—
strawberry jell-o flavored, cool-whip on top.
the sunflowers i bought for my mom watch me from the windowsill
as i gorge on forkfuls. this is quiet aftermath. this is coping with absence.
you're gone, yet i can't untie this from you—our birthday.
then as now, continents apart. there is crying. there is praying.
there is birth and pain and leaving and where is it we go from here?

MAN, EXPOSED.

like the undersides of leaves
before the rain, turned up
from all the humidity,
praising the storm, praising
the tension and static of
waiting as

the camera flash eats at
the shadow nestled against
his thigh—hanging figs,
cast purple by the night
invited by us into the
studio.

a poplar tree stretches up
to the sky, prostitute,
rising like hair along
the nape of a neck
that's been teased by a
finger,

and i notice the way his hand
drifts toward the missing
waistband of his briefs over
and over again, his forgetting

reminding me of its absence—

just outside, the trees sway their arms in tandem with the shutter's click. this distance: safety during the night in which i miss him most.

GOSPEL ACCORDING TO SAINT SEBASTIAN.

i.
is it fair
to be angry if he turns to wanting me,
the man whose face i covet,
body and all—should he love me
more than i love myself, a sacrament
i cannot satisfy.

ii.
it's like
the poor turning away the poor,
hoping that alone will bring us
into their circle of riches, make us
desirable beyond our own.

iii.
when i
imagine my body on his it is
blasphemous enough, a defilement
of a man fashioned in god's image.
lust and pride can be atoned,
but gluttony—no.

iv.
i loop
this rope around wrists. draw up,
suspend. call the archers to ready
and release, wanting to feel a likeness
of being prey, of being targeted
for the purpose of skinning,
reached inside, collected as bounty.
consumed.

v.
i sing.
arrows in my chest. singing as
my blood sprays upon his eyes,
restoring his sight, restoring
his distaste for me. and i am happy.

BEREAVEMENT: PART TWO.

tonight: the moon hides her face in her hands,
fistfuls of hair, the house dark with her,
dark as the eyes he uses to see the same sky
as mine. or so he says—swears it to me. tonight:
i could close my eyes and see just as little, a prolonged
blink, or eyes scrunched shut from stupor as
another's hands move down him like meteor showers,
more like an asteroid to me, leading to extinction.
but this is all guesswork. the nights have grown quiet
here, no more distant calls. something must have died,
or run underground in hiding. science gives me a theory:
survivors taking shape, how non-crabs become crabs
to the point of being near indistinguishable,
how there's a name for that process.

INCONSISTENCIES: NUMBER ONE.

february 29th was our first hiccup,
a day swallowed by an un-leap year,

which then swallowed our first
mensiversary, a month of dating,

almost as if it hadn't existed.
celebrating a day early would've felt

presumptuous, but waiting another
would've felt like losing faith.

we laughed about it. pretended
it meant something. hoped it didn't.

THE WATER BETWEEN US.

the river found us separated.
far from the church where lumber
had been laid to rest, forgotten, came
to stop the banks from running wild
while left alone. but the rains
were too much. it came to us,
crossed two continents for me,
an ocean for you, just to say:
i thought i knew you better.
its watered voice choking on litter
that'd been made by careless hands.
then receded. stained my white
shoes brown, smelling of the neolithic.

REHEARSED VISITATION.

i've not eaten in three days,
have not left this bed except to crawl
through the empty streets, to tour
the places better left forgotten.
here, where the river fed us in
the long night, where we made ourselves
into the sexless forms of children,
where no eyes could make us into whores,
as if we lacked the capacity for love.
where i'll dip my hands beneath the surface,
practicing the way in which i'll drift
my body down the river, aflame, alight,
imagining you already building another
city—our church made into sepulcher.

BETTER IS RELATIVE.

this fist in my throat is the
manifestation of my love for you.
breathing is strained, though not
impossible, like trying to love you
as only a friend would—doable,
but i feel my vision going.
hallucinations. breathing you in like
sweet air, your exhales. this is not
the death of love, but rather
its transformation. command these arms
to fly and i will sew feathers to them.
bid me come across the sea and i
will cut my neck and pray for gills,
for fins in place of feet, but ask me to
love you less and i'll refuse. i will not
deny this adaptation of the heart
in my chest to make room for yours.

FRESHENING.

in the mirror, i tug at the corners of my face
because you've seen it all, every inch of skin
and its many pores. and i want this for myself—
something that's never known you, quarantining
the parts exposed to your love and selfishness,
your need for uncompromised action, so i tear
my face away and the flies come, tracing the lines
you've long forgotten. the wind is cooler now,
sharper with the smallest bite, but it is new
and it is me in such a way that you'd never pick me
out in a police line-up: too red, you'd say. too fresh.

BEREAVEMENT: PART THREE.

a finch was discovered not long ago,
beak made perfect by wood, for wood,
and then came men and their axes and saws,
so it flew east, an ocean away. there it learned
softness, how to peck between cactus spines,
to drink as there were no trees. one finch
became so many as to warrant an exodus years later.
generations of thin-beaked finches,
having evolved toward softness. a party left
to forage for home before the rest took flight,
but they never came back. a few more flew west
in search of them, and came across the old land,
populated by trees as the men had died from
boredom and monotony. beneath the canopy,
at the bases of sequoias and elms, their little
broken bodies were found, beaks splintered
and shattered from the bark they tried to drink from.
when the search party returned, they didn't mention
death, only that the sea had swallowed the earth
and that population control was the sole solution—
that, and the planting of more cactus.

THE COMPLETE HISTORY OF US.

ends this day because i chose it to,
but does not end. continues on
like starfish without arms,
gerbils without tails after hawks
have grasped them out. this is not
a loss of self, despite how much
it feels like that. but my mind
should not be wandering
through men like air
despite the tug of my skin
toward yours, the movement
that feeds into this endless end:
ancient insects caught in amber.
dead dna. the moon violent
in her regular rise. raking
her fingers through the stars,
tossed them out and cast before
your feet and this is me regenerating.
replacing arm and tail. just me.
all me. watching you from afar.

INTERLUDE.

wading back home that summer night i came across ruins,
a temple, edges still sharp despite the smoothing mouth of time.

from the river i saw movement.

a mound of pale flesh and frills trickling in the moonlight,
axolotls as old as the hand-cut stones themselves.
watching me from the temple door, from within the pith
of all that's observed this land and all the lands before it.

servants of water. their eyes every cave and stream.

they climbed atop each other, formed a vague face,
blinked in unison, opened their soft mouths
and out swam the voices of all the men i've known.

together they chanted:
    forgive him, father, he knows not what we do.

INCONSISTENCIES: NUMBER THREE.

the distance expanded and contracted like lake ice.
first: only a few hours kept us clean and untangled,
the man before you—skin brown like yours.

this, i thought, *is no good, but good enough,* until i chased
him home to paraguay. it'd taken me eighteen hours
and three planes to do so. i had watched

the caribbean, pocked with the silhouettes of whales,
vanish into rainforest. moving in for the summer—
winter in the southern hemisphere—was transactional,

forced him to relocate his childhood toys, to make space
for my clothes. the man before you did this begrudgingly,
unaccustomed to sacrifice. his eyes turned over, inside out.

and now: your toys watch me from over your shoulder,
through the screen. you had assembled each one
by hand, and then put them on display, perched atop

the shelves that line your room. you're working on one now
as we speak, painting shadows into its plastic nooks, your lips
parted in focus, chancing me to stitch them together

with my own. but that would take a plane. money. a carry on.
so you and i try measuring the distance in months. it's a trick
i made for the nights of him before you—converting miles

into days for saving money, asking for permission,
praising the potential that the future holds while knowing
that none of it will come to pass, but it's fun to play with it,

roll the idea between fingers and mouths—a sinewy dream
we pretend is satisfying even with our mouths on other men.
for three months i shared the winter with the man before you—

balmier than any back home. when the summer passed,
he promised to follow me soon despite his plane to europe.
only four months. i had talked him down from nine.

his sister, too. but when he got there it doubled. tripled.
left me aching until i couldn't see him under the ice
anymore. my feet too light to break me through.

my mom says: *he's gone and so's his mind. men are everywhere.*
a friend says: *that boy did the same to me and my hopes.*
i've said goodbye. pruned the orchard of rot by hand,

and there you grow, an endearing shade of peach. so i eat
around the pit. suck juice from your flesh—sweet
as the early days of the man before you. but a little more punch.

more tangy than bitter. a slight aftertaste of his final hours with me, so i keep biting, savoring your skin against my lips. this, of course, is fantasy, but i swear i can taste you.

MEANING REVELATION OR UNVEILING.

the world is ending, the trees now rows of blackened matches.
the air's sole purpose: to fuel the roaring that tumbles down
the mountainside. yet the parrotlet can still be heard, so we stop
our running. turn and face this wall of flames. listen to the peeling
of organs, of meat from corpse by vultures: homeless, too—
and starving, pecking at the blisters on my arms, my ashened hair,
at the holes in my jeans, my tender knees. we lie down. tear off
our soot-covered clothes so we can fuck in its path. moaning with
the blaze, licking one another as the flames lick us, too, stealing flesh
from bone until we are just two skeletons rattling in a mockery of sex.
this is nothing new to us. the vultures have long gone, and we
are consumed by the end—only fragments remaining.

VIVISECTION.

you wake up in a morgue,
the clean cold stinging
your parts that kiss the metal.
you've been stripped bare,
an incision drawn and sewn
down your axis. the skin puckered,
not bleeding. and then i'm there,
eyes goggled, hands gloved
in black rubber—smelling like tires
in summer. i take the two of them
and pop open the sutures,
dig inside, slip past the ribs
and the muscles hugged by fascia,
searching for something honest.
but you've been emptied out.
nothing left to give, the air
thick with blood and hesitation.
i'd hoped for something soft,
untouched, as pink
as the day it was knitted
in your mother.

ENTRY FOR TRAUMA RELIVED.

i saw him on campus again. today: he wore
that red stocking hat, still plaid, still snug
against his head. my eyes fixed forward.

after passing, i reasoned he could've been
anyone else. i'd gone years without a sighting,
without thinking any slight resemblance
was him that night on top of me.

someone said he'd taken up coke,
replaced the blunts, lived in the frat house
where others had been raped—drunk, too.
had private bodies treated like willing earth.
raked with fingers, ones only he could have.

i hid in the bathroom. i heard three men
enter. each one him. each one
reminded me that privacy isn't guaranteed.
it's granted. permitted. as i left the urinal
i turned and saw him—the brown eyes
that drifted from mine the night
he climbed off my drunken body,
said he couldn't fuck me crying.

he passed into the stall, rolled off of me.
i made time to wash my hands,
to glance briefly at the mirror.

SEEDS & SKIN.

yes,

i let that man settle inside me.
age like cider. honeycrisp.

all this sweating: a fever
                 an outward expression
of the men i've swallowed,
                 the fear i've swallowed
                 since meeting him.

is like my silence—
caused by fermentation.

and yet I want to press my tongue
                 into him, rip it from his body.
present this dying torso
                 which for him I have prepared.
kiss him softly on the neck.

call him *daddy*.

INCONSISTENCIES: NUMBER TWO.

it goes a little something like this:
boy meets boy through the internet,
separated by an estimated 1,600 miles—
some 2,550 kilometers. they prefer
to think of the former even though
there is no difference.

let's start cleaner:
boy meets boy with no chance
of meeting, so they swap naked
pictures, compliments, screens, wishes,
the pillars and domes of their bodies.

but if we're being honest:
this is going to hurt. the nurse lied.
the music lied. love can't cross
rivers and freeways because this
isn't love—can't be. too fresh and
nothing more than little guesses.
plus, one boy tried it for a year
and ended it the night they met.

when we get to the end:
one boy will have had sex over the weekend
and thought of him, held him

like a communion wafer—dry
in the mouth, thin. today they'll make plans
for dates, even pick out the places.

now, between conversations:
there is silence. little-to-no wondering
about the other because there
are friends. sushi. obligations outside
of them. that time one got drunk
and the other high. confessed
their bodies through the phone.
eyes bleary. throats burnt by the rough
taste of distance. suspended there,
far in the back, beyond a finger's reach.

I'LL NAME HER SOMETHING SOFT.

it took two days for the next man to enter, started
with an out of town visit—the two-hour commute
giving me time to wonder if i should just drive
on through, or sleep in my car instead.

but i went, and it reminded me that all men taste the same.
warm and guarded. slightly salty. the flavor and scent
clung to me throughout the night while he slept,
earlier complaining of the same, though this payoff
is better than wet mouths on untouched skin,
knowing that i was capable of getting over you quickly,
capable of allowing myself to get over you quickly.

i like to think that i didn't use him for that epiphany.
he offered me a bed in transit and i took him
up on it. before sleep, we discussed work, how his dog—
wheezing at the foot of the bed as french bull dogs do—
creeps, has seen every man come and go from that room.
i spent some time at the edge of dozing looking up adoption
shelters, the price of litter, the watching habits of cats.

LOCKJAW.

he tells me there's a bird
for every fountain here,
and a color for every summer
and boy who would snap you
in half with just a look.

but if beauty is pain
then looking is agony,
and seeing him now
under the bar lights,
i can feel it: the curling back
of my fingernails, each
popping off without blood,
and the steady dive of a needle
into my tender heel
'til it scratches bone—

and this is what i call *atonement* or
appreciating a body that's not my own.

i take another drink, watch
him name some birds:
cecilia. sofia. anastasia.
all saints worth praying to,
though it's hard knowing why

when drunk, when trying to imagine
the color of his summer
or understand how he remembers
each bird he names when there
are just as many fountains
for tossing pennies, for pressing wishes
against their tense surfaces—
the color of opal,
of rain-wet wings in flight,
the color of his summer.

and there it is: right behind my eye,
where scar tissue and astigmatism
smudge him, struggling to make
his face out of darkness.

i'm tongue-deep in a bottle
of cider. rejected his wine
because even the sweet stuff's
too tart. the waitress brings
another one, sets it down
so it can bleed out on
the coaster, and she shoulders
my wet hesitation.

he names another bird
just to remember me
when he's sober, and yes—

this makes my jaw feel
like locking up, soft tissues
ossifying into bone to hold back
and clench the teeth.

ask to take his hand.
ask to grow his mother into loving.

this is what the bottles whisper
as i rest my hot head
on the wooden counter,
occupy these thoughts
with my tongue against my gums,
the seams of my teeth.

i rise up. look at him again.
pop a backbone into place.

between the bricks and mortar,
humidity seeps in, wrapping us up
with the late-night fog
of expiration. our friends have finished
their drinks, and so we're retched
back out into the city—
our planes de-iced and humming.

TEA LEAF APOSTLE.

that night in the coffee shop:
i read you in the tea leaves
right before your eyes, un-brown,
and you pulled back. turned up your nose
at divination, though acknowledged it
all the same, nodded as if i weren't
drawing blood, peeling back your skin
as my dad had taught me with fish, saying:
don't waste your time. ignore the way they squirm.
i gestured, asking if i could touch you, too—
hope for healing.

the coffee shop was ablaze with chatter
and the clacking of keyboards.
you itched your nose, blamed it on the air,
later confessed it psychosomatic—
your body's defense against being known,
against knowing itself too well.
rejecting this wrong kind of entry.

and so you said:
don't touch me there, not yet, maybe never.
i haven't worked the kinks out.
they're a jumbled mess of tendons and heartstrings
he rearranged, like the insides of the man

he'd fuck on wednesdays, fridays, too,
when i was out, hunched over the night.

maybe it was your eyes, your beard,
the way you spoke honestly to me
yet dishonestly to yourself. it made me
brazen. imagined kissing you outside
despite the redness of your nose.
i thought to show it off, so i drew lines
between us: our bad ex-boyfriends—
yours worse than mine, but better
in bed and better at leaving.

and to call hope a feathered thing is wrong—
its body's a serpent, long and coiled,
seething at the smallest scent of heat,
something of yours i couldn't latch onto,
couldn't remember if you smelled more
like juniper or leather, so i hoped for balsam.

GROWTH RATE.

i take these tweezers, black.
slip the four long hairs, black too,
from their follicles, nestled
within the birthmark that mirrors
the one my aunt has,
though on the opposite arm,
and i wonder how often she plucks
them, washes them down the sink,
forgets they were even there until
one day, in the bath, she sees them
fully grown, reminded of how they
protrude like a mosquito's mouth.
i haven't spoken to her in months,
not since she prayed for my deliverance
from the red-breath rooms of men.
she's yet to apologize,
and i've yet to stop plucking,
sucking, calling out a man's name
while kneeling, too.

PINK.

the piercer hovers
above me like regret
and slips the hollow needle
through the dip
of my nose.
pain unfurls across
my face, slow as
moonlight cactus.

have you been pierced here before?
he asks, eyes on me,
purposefully away from
the cow's head bleeding
down at my feet.

*no, my pores are large
like my dad's.*

the white gold hoop
slides in easily.
he asks me of
the placement.
too late to go back now
i say.

next week: on
my brother's couch
i'm straddling a man
who's balding like
my dad has,
the man's hips crushed
between my thighs, faces
like glacier against earth.

the morning after:
my nose rejected him.
granuloma. keloid. unsure
of the proper name yet
pink all the same, once
inside now blooming out.
the notorious bump,
trying to swallow up
what's foreign.

dad says they're all pink
inside. he says this
of women. he doesn't know
that men are pink,
too, especially when
you dig deep enough.

MILK SETTLES ON THE TONGUE.

silence does the body good.
the taste of milk, held in my mouth,
changes, carries with itself tones
of earth and my ancestors
teaching themselves to break it down
when no crops could grow.
and i've inherited the product
of their plight without having fought
for it. yet i fight for you,
for your words when they've gone
for a day or two. sex always brings you
back from that distant mist.
but there are moments of clarity,
times when you comment on it—
apologize. when you say:
there are plenty of places in florida
i haven't seen, and it's implied
that you mean those guarded
by water steeped in cattails
and those things only gators could eat.
those places populated by people
like my father. but at least
those places sing. i know
because we have them here in spirit,
and they're always coughing

up sound. the sour taste
of pond water replaces that of milk
in my mouth. come here now, babe,
and teach me how creatures
in the bayou move through water.

GIFTING MY FATHER A SECOND BIRTH.

my grandmother says there was a blizzard the first time,
my father born to snow drifts, slush stained pink.
the smell of iron lost to the wind that whipped them.

i was born in haste: cord detached, breached. ripping
myself from my mother before my given time.
but there was light. doctors. my father straight from work.

now it's his turn. i flick the lights out. unplug the fridge.
practice eating only honeydew and brine.
when the day comes, there's a pressure between

my lungs. had felt nothing those prior months, feared
he'd gone to stone inside me, but he was crowning.
crying. breaking through my swollen body.

thrashing into the world anew. here i have made him
into my own image—incubated an extra week
to enlarge the heart. extra care. sensitive labor.

chickadees calling in the morning, my body folding inward.
finished. i reach for him, curled upon the floor, bleeding
without wounds. slide open his eyes, expecting brown and there—

white. the tissue singed in transit. held too close. damaged
by the heat of me: low but long. no use for a heart
with no eyes to see. i stuff him back inside. pray for delivery.

FALLEN.

in this, our only sanctuary,
where our blood won't stain
the sidewalks or a freshly washed
t-shirt, i can hold his hand.
leave my eyes to rest.
let the air between us
become shoulders.

fables of a modern world.
re-making it like desperate gods
only wanting to praise each other,
to have a temple no greater
than a birdhouse. but so what if we do?
one day his wings will grow
wider than a robin's, and i
will build him such a house,
a proper place for worship.
self-serving as any god,
and in need of protection.

this has precedence. not the first time
an iconoclast with a rifle aimed
at heaven, at self-made gods
of a world that'd rather see vacant skies.
vacant shrines. tombs of waiting.

gods converted to myth despite
the thunder, the screaming of our bodies
falling like hailstones,
like lightning with the rain.

then make this our last testament to living,
as a vengeful pantheon.
a flood contested and all-too-soon
forgotten, to wipe clean the sin
of visibility, of sound.
we'll bury ourselves on impact,
covered in dirt and stardust,
burial shrouds. veils
for the weddings we'll never have.

APOSTASY:
INSTRUCTIONS FOR GETTING OVER ME.

i.   take a match to your mouth
and burn away the alcohol of my kiss.
do not protect the surrounding tissue
with vaseline. let it scorch you, hurt you
as a blistered and peeling sunburn does.

ii.   surround yourself with men, or don't.
but i prefer them, circling me
like sharks, or cars in a parking lot,
looking for an opening, a flash of lights
in reverse. something to beat others to.

iii.   when you let the next one in,
don't let him go too deep, don't do it
uncovered, unguarded. it'll be like pressing
salted fingers into a slow-mending wound
in the shape of me. don't let it tear.

iv.   masturbate to the songs we used
to make love to. if you cry—keep going.
if you don't—stop. turn the music up
louder, 'til the walls shake and the bass
rattles your chest. eat a pineapple.

v.   erase my numbers—all of them.
         my phone. my birthday. my height, both
         the real one and the official one.
         the date of the anniversary we'll never
         have. my phone passcode. my favorites.

vi.   keep the photos and videos i sent you,
         but not too long, just enough to learn
         how to cum without thinking of me,
         'til you start to see the purple stretchmarks
         and the curves of my body that love had hidden.

vii.   ask your sister to lend you her eyes
         to see me as she does: without romance
         or sexual body. this will expedite the process
         should you stay true to our pact: to stay friends
         no matter what, despite ourselves.

viii.   be honest with yourself. the eggs were burnt.
         my eyes never the right shade of blue.
         my body always taking up too much space.
         i snored. would touch the thermostat.
         cried over nothing. needed medication.

ix.   i promise you'll see how it was long over
         before it was made evident to you.
         this will not be the sweetest solace,
         but it will do. when the moment comes,

        trap it in a jar, a firefly for your nightstand.

x.   realize that i've already touched another man.
        imagine it: the lips you kissed wrapped
        around a stranger. make the image your mantra,
        your visual prayer. *hail mary, full of grace.*
        the devil was with me, inside me, and i him.

LIMINAL SPACES.

river: watch us now in return. see us standing here
in the window-light, thirsting at the shimmer of your skin,
how you carry cafés and hotels like ours along your sides.

earlier, he and i had argued about hallways, the color
of espresso on wood, and lives we've yet to live,
will never live, could only live if timing had been right,

if constellations and conditions could favor us.
but he was born to a liminal space—cusp between
aries and pisces, ram and fish, fire and water—

and i, libra, rise from the air and admire you, watered beast,
rolling beneath the bridge, aflame with the light of living.
tell me this is all but new. tell me this is storybook and history.

for now: there are currents, snaps between neurons. impulses
to close the distance and see what his boyfriend knows
of touching him when sun's been tucked away.

but this, the world, is just a hallway made for passing through.
i cry at this, my luck, and he attempts a counter—gestures
at the city, saying *there's just so much to see.*

and so i say *too much for just one man or country.*
the lilacs on the window ledge are bleeding out tonight.
their perfume stains my lungs, but will be forgotten

on the plane ride home when he too is packed and off to
a familiar destination, to the man who waits for him bathed
in hallway light, ready for that known bed,

dropping bags on floors and i swear i'll feel it when
he climbs between the sheets to hold him as he holds him
now before my eyes—in quiet, in memory, in loving secret.

INCONSISTENCIES: NUMBER SIX.

he found them sleeping
in the dirt, winged emeralds,
the cicadas from his memories.

he spent three days
searching for them all,
clawed his way
through neighbors' yards
just to be sure.

their song still buzzed
in his mind. ears
hungry for the lullaby
the bugs hadn't sung
in seven years—when he last
could be found excavating
his past lover's mouth,
framed by a beard
and questions of wickedness.

he brought the insects
water, light, the warmth
of his bed at night,
nestled against his chest.

he did this long.
he did this urgently patient.

nine months
and they'd lost their color,
twelve shades darker,
their tiny heartbeats
softened and slowed.

he tried to eat them up,
hoping to swallow
their song, make melody
his memory
in the morning light,
but no music came.

only handfuls
had been spared
by the elasticity of his
stomach—its limits.

so he laid them back to rest
beneath an oak
by the river, seemingly dead,
and sat himself down
for a great long while.

it took two years
and a heavy rain
to coax them out,
but their song
had turned to melancholy,
a call of wondering,
of searching and loss,

and this reminded him
too much of the man
he'd loved those summers past.

he scooped them up
by silent dozens
and plunged them in
the river deep,
sang their saddest song,
cried, didn't stop
until all their bodies
floated still and away.

at home that night,
his stomach thrummed
with the confused song
of the cicadas
he'd swallowed,
their song the same
as those before.

the man drank in
the river until
it was a memory, too,
yet the song continued,
he continued,
the moonrise breeze
making laughter
out of grass.

PRAYER FOR SAINT KATHIE.

mom: grant me the serenity of getting over him. grant me
love, commitment, sex—in that exact order. peace
when i look in the mirror before leaving. hope
when the two of us finally meet. strength to undress myself
before his eyes—brown like those of all i loved.
grant me tongue and teeth and words to fill the silence,
the open air between us, and the canyon carved out
by the love that came before him. grant me good memories
of that river. grant me eyes just for him. mid-morning
phone calls. tea and coffee in the bitter afternoons.
grant me his well-kept nails and his lips good for kissing.
in-laws for him and for me to see us in and out of doors—
an emphasis on *in*. grant him a lover who can comb out
anxieties and make eggs unburnt. keep venom from my mouth
when things get hasty. mom: i ask you to grant me these things
because you made me. gave me life. crafted all these cells
that keep me going through replication—constant birth
and death—and that's the closest to god i've ever been.

SÉANCE.

this house has a habit of snagging those who pass through it
regardless of death, whether aggravated or a slow exhale.

and i've grown so tired of the company. in the morning: i wake
to communing murmurs, the recycled thuds of footsteps above.

later: i catch the scent of someone half-forgotten before it dissolves
back into air. an echo, i think, stuck in the threads of my clothing.

in the kitchen, the cabinets are always found open, pans and bowls
        strew
out like tombstones in a hasty cemetery, and i blame the open window.

after two years, i acknowledge them.

my fingers are spread, palms sweating. hands on the dark blue velvet
that clings to the table beneath. i close my eyes, open my chest.

i'm stitched inside a dead man's suit—too tight in the arms and
        shoulders,
leaving me hunched, but i do not struggle, do not dare itch at the seams.

i'm holding council with ghosts in my living room. the lights are out
and i'm calling them forward to find a reason for their persistence.

when they speak i become aware of all the bones inside me, how they ache
like my mom's before a storm blows in, like divining is woven into our marrow.

LIGHT IN THE STAIRWELL.

i know what moonlight can be, how to capture it in a jar.
let me teach you—like this. then we shatter them
on the basement floor. a disco dream. all my almost lovers
dancing on the shards in heaps with feet still clean, uncut.
the music is this: our hungry sobs of loneliness and jealousy.
flying through the air. black witch moths nipping at our ears.
when we grow too tired and light comes flooding down,
i trip up the stairs, crawling on hands and knees to him—
head bowed, palms rubbed raw by carpets and praying.

his eyes thick with frost, away, guided from me and toward
the sky. i see the sun is coming. his ochre skin awash with
its honesty—revelations soft as thunder, so i drink
from the stars again, my belly hot and churning.

the assumption of my crush at the edge of the horizon
hurts. love seems to always end this way, with another's
hands, and then begins, or at least confuse it for a moment.

there was a time when streetlights would eat away
the pregnant darkness of the city square, leave
the two of us to make men's faces out of shadows,
a show-and-tell. *he slapped me here. loved me here.
said this was his favorite spot to lick and kiss and turn
my body inside out.* the deer would come then, wearing

their little masks, snouts black and wet from morning.

and now: my almost lover soars above me, eyes
locked tight upon the constellations that run past
the sleeping moon, drained to black, exhausted from watching
me and all my others. maybe this feeling is acceptance
or shame in slow motion for taking each other's bodies
in stride. suddenly he is every man, every spine i traced
with my patient tongue—or had hoped to.

and i give them to you for safe-keeping, despite
my inflicted wounds. despite how they carved me up
with all their wanting. shepherd them toward the heavens,
each a star in his own right yet placed within a constellation.
never lonely, as no lines can be drawn by a single point,
no myths made to cope with memory and full disclosure.

so let me name this a dream: the caving of my chest.
the bloody snow. the skin i wear that just won't fit the same
after having their hands between it. i slip out. leave myself
without goodbye, to be found by someone else,
given up for scavengers and squatters. reborn between the drifts.

POSTLUDE.

getting home was never enough,
        never less than an excused escape.

rational distance from all the construction work
we'd left for a summer we knew wouldn't come.

it's in this old familiar air that i find you
        by the water's edge that's come and gone

as you have, but has all now returned
        in different form—with quieter edges.

this bed of mine is weighted by our sweat,
        our slumber, our secrets that the owls in the attic

tended to while i was off and away, chasing you,
        chasing any man who promised me a shared drink.

tonight: the stars are still eating at my insides,
        love, and i have received this in myself,

the due penalty of loving a hoped-for you
        with pressure building within my capillaries.

when you come back with a different face,
      ready to try again, to cross the swollen threshold,

i say to you: *ask and it will be given to you.*
      search, and you will find. knock, and the door

will be opened for you. you weigh this in each hand,
      slipping fingers between my ribs, imagine doing so with

your teeth, your tongue, whispering *novena*
      into my neck when you finally decide to enter me.

NOTES

The concept of "the long night" was lifted from *Game of Thrones*.

hymn for brown-eyed boys.
The line "same song, second verse" is taken from the title of a poem by Rebecca Gayle Howell.

we inherited their mistakes.
The line "cast me out into the sleeping bodies / of pigs" references the book of Luke. The line "that land without evil" references a Guaraní myth.

séance.
The line "i'm holding council with ghosts in my living room" is inspired by the song *Prodigal Son* by Rationale.

gifting my father a second birth.
Inspired by the collection *Teaching My Mother How to Give Birth* by Warsan Shire.

interlude.
Inspired by the short story *Axolotl* by Julio Cortázar. References Luke 23:34.

meaning revelation or unveiling.
Title inspired by the Book of Revelation.

inconsistencies: number two.
The line "it goes a little something like this" is inspired by the poem *Peanuts and Dirty Biker Bars (Compassions IV)* by Merkin Karr.

apostasy: instructions for getting over me.
References the Catholic prayer *Hail Mary*.

light in the stairwell.
References the song *The Light in the Piazza* from the musical of the same name, both in its title and the line "i know what moonlight can be." The lines "revelations soft as thunder" and "taking each other's bodies / in stride" reference the song *I Dreamed a Dream* from the musical *Les Misérables*.

postlude.
References Romans 1:26-27 and Matthew 7:7. The usage of the word "novena" is inspired by the book of the same name by Jacques J. Rancourt.

Acknowledgements

fallen.
What Rough Beast, Indolent Books

men to my father.
HIV Here and Now, Indolent Books

inconsistencies: number three.
Periphery Literary & Arts Journal

seeds & skin.
HIV Here and Now, Indolent Books

lockjaw.
Levee Magazine

GRATITUDES

Before anyone else, I must thank my parents, Kathie and Kyle, for pushing me toward my greatest self, for gifting me a love of the unknown, for making me a sponge, for supporting and loving me in the face of difference. Thank you to Kolby, Bailey, and Mason for inspiring me and drawing me home. The same thanks should be extended to my grandparents, my aunts, my uncles, my cousins, my ancestors—both by blood and through identity—for clearing the brush so that I might pave my own way. Thanks to my friends for motivating and encouraging me: Kelley Lewis-Fox, Vilune Sestokaite, Trevor Guinn, Laura Gil-Echeverria, Tracey Lien, Hannah Soyer, Nadine Worley, Eric Orosco, Kara Knickerbocker, Erin Verbick, and countless others. Thanks to those who helped me shape this book in classrooms: Kennia Lopez, Bailey Weese, Richard Sonnenmoser, and Luke Rolfes. To Megan Kaminski—for being a magical advisor, for seeing some of these poems in rougher forms and accepting me into the MFA program at KU, for bringing light—thank you. Without a doubt, the people at Indolent Books, especially Michael Broder and Robert Carr, are to thank for helping me shape this manuscript into something beautiful with their trust, care, and feedback. To the men whose impacts and interactions I wrote about within these poems, I thank you and hope life is treating you kindly. Lastly, thank you to the great people at Rebel Satori Press and QueerMojo; because of you, these songs will last long after the night has faded and the sun has come.

www.ingramcontent.com/pod-product-compliance
Lightning Source LLC
Chambersburg PA
CBHW051349040426
42453CB00007B/482